How to Solve
Math Word Problems
Step-by-Step

Happy Frog Press

Copyright 2020 by Janine Toole PhD

All rights reserved. This book or any portion thereof may not be reproduced or used in any manner whatsoever without the express written permission of the publisher except for the use of brief quotations in a book review.

First Printing, 2020

ISBN 9798566752402

Table of Contents

Introduction	5

Part 1 Learn	7

Part 2 Practice	55

Part 3 Extend	73

Introduction

Welcome to **How to Solve Math Word Problems**.

This workbook teaches your learner how to understand and solve word problems involving addition and subtraction. The workbook is specifically designed for learners who struggle with word problems.

In Part 1, students are introduced to a foolproof, five-step process for solving word problems. The process is taught incrementally with lots of practice problems to build your learner's skill and confidence. In addition, clear instructions and lots of whitespace make this book appealing to struggling students

Part 2 contains practice problems to build proficiency. Finally, Part 3 provides extension tasks where your learner uses their new skills to create new word problems.

Get started right now and give your learner the skills they need to succeed at math!

Part 1

Learning

Teacher Notes

In Part 1, your student learns a 5-step process for completing an addition or subtraction word problem.

The steps are:

1. Understand the question
2. Identify what you already know
3. Seek out clue words
4. Draw a model with numbers
5. Write and solve the equation

Step 1: Understand the Question

The first step in solving a math word problem is to understand the question. The question tells you what information you need to find out.

To find the question, look for the sentence that ends with a question mark '?'.

Your first task will be to underline the question in each of the following word problems. Here's an example.

Underline the question.

John has 3 blue marbles and 6 green marbles. <u>How many marbles does John have altogether?</u>

This is the question!

Understand the Question 1

Underline the question in each word problem.

Mary started with $7 and spent $4. How much money does she have left? £3.00

Amy and Brian collected shells on the beach. Amy found 5 shells and Brian found 7 shells. How many shells did they collect altogether? 12 shells

A restaurant sold 4 salty snacks and 3 sweet snacks. How many snacks did the restaurant sell in all? 7

When Kiera went to bed, there were 7 birds on the lake. When she woke up, there were only 3 birds. How many birds left during the night? 4

Understand the Question 1

Underline the question in each word problem.

On Sunday, Carol read in her room to pass the time. She read 6 comic books in the morning and 2 novels in the afternoon. How many books did she read during the day?   8

A treasure hunter discovered a buried treasure chest. She opened it up and discovered that it contained 5 diamonds and 3 rubies. How many gems were in the chest?   8

Carl built a cabin with 12 logs, and his friend Dora built a cabin with 15 logs. How many more logs did Dora use?   3

Understand the Question 2

Now you know how to find the question. Next, select the option which could be the real answer to the word problem.

A fruit stall has sold 5 bags of oranges and 3 bags of apples. How many bags of fruit has the stall sold?

> The stall has sold 5 bags of oranges.

> The stall has sold 8 bags of fruit.

David has 10 toys. 4 are stuffed animals and the rest are action figures. How many action figures does David have?

> David has six action figures.

> David has six stuffed animals.

Understand the Question 2

For each question, select the response that could be the real answer.

On a school trip to a farm, Ellen saw three lambs and five goats. How many animals did Ellen see?

Ellen saw 8 animals. ✓

Ellen saw five goats.

At the end of the day, the bakery had five cakes left. They started with ten cakes at the beginning of the day. How many cakes did the bakery sell?

The bakery sold five cakes. ✓

The bakery started with ten cakes.

Understand the Question 2

For each question, select the response that could be the real answer.

Ernie planted twenty flowers, but three of them died. How many flowers does Ernie have now?

| Ernie has 17 flowers. ✓ |

| Ernie lost three flowers. |

A teacher has ten students in her class. Three of them are boys. How many girls are in the class?

| There are seven students in the class. |

| There are seven girls in the class. ✓ |

Understand the Question 2

For each question, select the response that could be the real answer.

Fred saw 7 big fish and 12 small fish at the aquarium. How many fish did he see in total?

Fred saw 19 fish. ✓

Fred saw 19 big fish.

Freya has six red pencils and four blue pencils. How many more red pencils than blue pencils does she have?

Freya has 2 more red pencils. ✓

Freya has 10 red pencils altogether.

8/9/22

Understand the Question 2

For each question, select the response that could be the real answer.

Greg colored six stars blue and seven stars red. How many stars did he color?

> Greg colored 13 yellow stars.

> Greg colored 13 stars. ✓

Gina has $10.00. She spends $3.00 on snacks. How much money does she have left?

> Gina has $10.00 at the beginning.

> Gina has $7.00 left. ✓

Understand the Question 3

For each question, write out what the answer will look like, using a space '_____' for the number. The first one has been done for you.

John had 3 blue marbles and 6 green marbles. How many marbles does John have altogether?

John has __9__ marbles altogether.

Adriana caught seven fish and gave three to her friend. How many fish does Adriana have left?

4

Understand the Question 3

For each question, write out what the answer will look like, using a space '_____' for the number.

Lincoln borrowed three books from the library and also borrowed five books from his friend. How many books did Lincoln borrow altogether? 8

Nadia was paddling a canoe. She paddled six times on the left and five times on the right. How many times did she paddle in all? 11

Understand the Question 3

For each question, write out what the answer will look like, using a space '_____' for the number.

Sam bought seven red bean bags and gave one of them to his friend. How many bean bags does Sam have left?

6

The recipe needs one cup of brown sugar and two cups of white sugar. How many cups of sugar are needed in total? *3*

Understand the Question 3

For each question, write out what the answer will look like, using a space '_____' for the number.

Nyah wrote three hundred words. Her essay must contain 500 words. How many more words does she have to write?   200

Oliver picked ten strawberries and gave three to his brother. How many does he have left?   7

Step 2: Identify What You Already Know

The second step in understanding a math word problem is to identify the information that is given to you.

To do this, you find the numbers that are mentioned in the word problem. The numbers might be digits like '5' or words like 'five'.

Here's an example.

Underline the numbers that are given in the word problem.

John has 3 blue marbles and 6 green marbles. How many marbles does John have altogether?

Identify What You Already Know 1

Underline the numbers that are given in the word problem.

Liam took five books to school but only brought three home. How many books did he leave at school?

2

Hattie built a house with 3 red blocks, 5 blue blocks and 7 yellow blocks. How many bricks did Hattie use to build her house?

15

Sam planted ten seeds. Seven of them sprouted. How many did not sprout?

3

Identify What You Already Know 1

Underline the numbers that are given in the word problem.

In one week, Ian drank three glasses of vanilla milk and four glasses of chocolate milk. How many glasses of milk did he drink?

Nine children came to Dino's party. Seven were boys. How many girls came to the party?

Lisa is training for a race. Last week she ran five miles. This week she ran two miles more than that. How many miles did she run this week?

Identify What You Already Know 2

What information does the word problem tell you? Write your answer in bullet form. The first one is done for you.

John has 3 blue marbles and 6 green marbles. How many marbles does John have altogether?

- John has 3 blue marbles
- John has 6 green marbles

Mike took seven books from the shelf and then returned three. How many books does he have left?

4

Identify What You Already Know 2

What information does the word problem tell you?
Write your answer in bullet form.

Ivan sold six balloons on Tuesday and eight balloons on Wednesday. How many balloons did he sell on Tuesday and Wednesday? *14*

Jenna finished the race in 5 minutes. Jack finished the race in six minutes. Who took the longest?

Identify What You Already Know 2

What information does the word problem tell you?
Write your answer in bullet form.

Kayleigh found three beetles and two worms in the garden. How many animals did Kayleigh find?

5

Liam read five pages in the morning and nine pages in the afternoon. How many more pages did he read in the afternoon?

four

Identify What You Already Know 2

What information does the word problem tell you?
Write your answer in bullet form.

Leanne found ten marbles and gave three to her sister. How many marbles does Leanne have left?

7

Maria played chess 5 times on Saturday and 3 times on Sunday. How many times did she play chess on the weekend?

Eight

Identify What You Already Know 2

What information does the word problem tell you?
Write your answer in bullet form.

Ten people were on the bus. Five people got off at the next stop. How many people are left on the bus?

Naomi's tower is seven blocks tall. She adds four more blocks. How tall is her tower now?

Step 3:
Look for Clue Words

The third step in understanding a math word problem is to identify clue words. Clue words help you figure out whether you need to add or subtract.

Here are some clue words.

Addition Clue Words	Subtraction Clue Words
Combined Increased Total Sum Added to Together Plus Add	Minus Less than Less Fewer than Difference Decreased Take away More than Left How many more

Look For Clue Words 1

Underline the clue words in the word problem. The first one is done for you.

John has 3 blue marbles and 6 green marbles. How many marbles does John have <u>altogether</u>?

Patty needs to draw seven flowers. She has drawn five. How many does she have left to draw?

Olivia has three books and Pierre has five. How many more books does Pierre have than Olivia?

Joy has three cakes and Fred has two more than Joy. How many cakes does Fred have?

Look For Clue Words 1

Underline the clue words in the word problem.

Priya has seven cookies and Leo has twelve. How many fewer cookies does Priya have?

Priya has seven cookies and Leo has twelve. How many cookies do they have in total?

Gina put three cups of flour in the bowl. Then she added two more. How many cups did she put in the bowl altogether?

Liam has two cars and Lisa has ten. What is the sum of their cars?

Look For Clue Words 2

Look at the clue words and decide whether you should do addition or subtraction.

Hattie read three pages and Henry read two pages. How many pages did they read altogether?

> Addition

> Subtraction

Hattie read three pages and Henry read two pages. What is the difference in the number of pages they read?

> Addition

> Subtraction

Look For Clue Words 2

Look at the clue words and decide whether you should do addition or subtraction.

Mike bought five candies and gave three of them to his sister. How many candies does Mike have left?

Addition

Subtraction

Marissa earned $5 for babysitting and $3 for dog walking. How much did she earn in total?

Addition

Subtraction

Look For Clue Words 2

Look at the clue words and decide whether you should do addition or subtraction.

Rosa sold six lemonades and two sweet teas at her lemonade stand. How many drinks did she sell in all?

Addition

Subtraction

Neville planted three seeds and Nancy planted five seeds. How many fewer seeds did Neville plant?

Addition

Subtraction

Step 4
Draw A Model With Numbers

The fourth step in solving a math word problem is to sketch a quick representation or model of the problem and put in the information you know. This process really helps you understand the problem.

Your drawing does not have to be neat. A quick sketch is all that is needed.

Here's an example.

John has 3 blue marbles and 6 green marbles. How many marbles does John have altogether?

??? How many altogether?

6 green	3 blue

Let's look at another example to see how to do this.

John has 10 marbles. 4 are green. How many are not green?

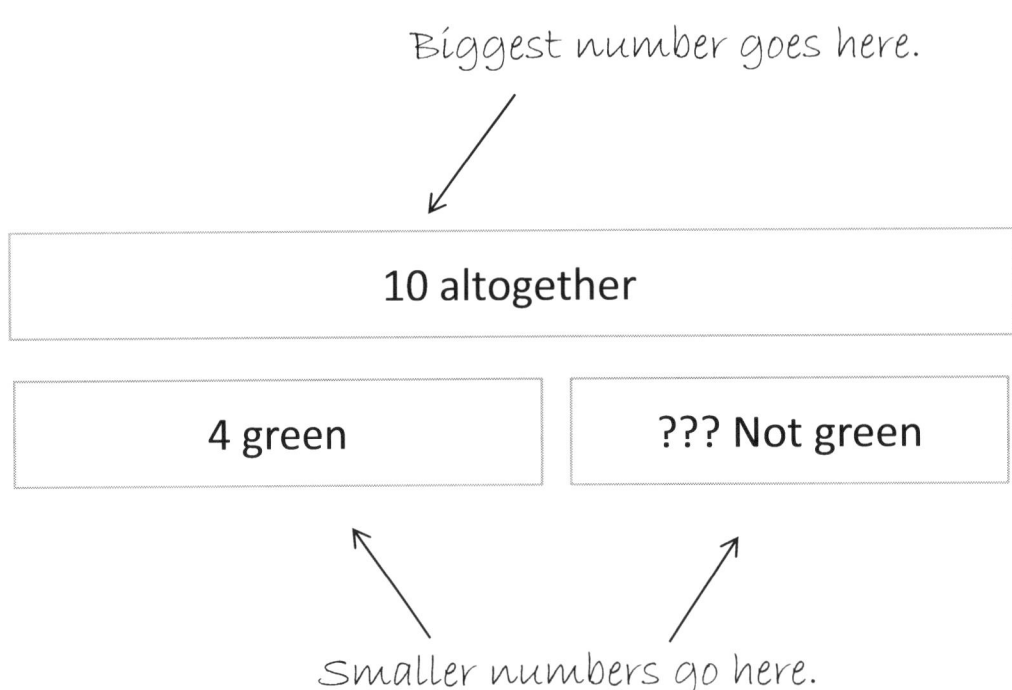

Use your understanding of the problem to figure out which is the biggest number and which are the smaller numbers. The smaller numbers can go in either of the smaller boxes.

Draw A Model With Numbers

Do a quick drawing to represent what you know so far.

Callie found five oak leaves and six maples leaves. How many leaves did she find in total?

Draw A Model With Numbers

Do a quick drawing to represent what you know so far.

Reece ate ten crackers on Monday and five crackers on Tuesday. How many crackers did he eat in all?

Draw A Model With Numbers

Do a quick drawing to represent what you know so far.

Sarah played ten games of tennis. She won five games. How many games did she not win?

Draw A Model With Numbers

Do a quick drawing to represent what you know so far.

Ramona saw three ducks in the morning and seven swans in the afternoon. How many more swans than ducks did she see?

Draw A Model With Numbers

Do a quick drawing to represent what you know so far.

Aidan saw three cars and eight trucks drive by his house. How many vehicles did he see in all?

Draw A Model With Numbers

Do a quick drawing to represent what you know so far.

Five blocks fell from the table to the floor. Six are left on the table. How many blocks were on the table to start with?

Step 5
Write & Solve the Equation

The last step in solving a math word problem is to figure out what math operation is needed to find the information you are asked for. You do this by looking at your model and thinking about the clue words you found. For example:

John has 3 blue marbles and 6 green marbles. How many marbles does John have <u>altogether</u>?

??? How many altogether?

6 green	3 blue

The equation is:

How Many Altogether = 6 + 3

Let's look at another example.

John has 10 marbles. 4 are green. How many are not green?

Here's our model.

10 altogether

4 green	??? not green

The equation:

$$\text{Number Not Green} = 10 - 4$$

You are now ready to try this for yourself!

Write & Solve the Equation 1

Choose the correct equation. Use the blank space to work through the word problem steps. In this first problem, the model is drawn for you.

Logan ate three apples and two oranges. How many pieces of fruit did he eat altogether?

??? How many altogether?

3 apples	2 oranges

Total Fruit = 3 + 2

Total Fruit = 3 - 2

Write & Solve the Equation 1

Choose the correct equation. Use the blank space to work through the word problem steps.

Sarah bought five candies and Laura bought three more candies than Sarah. How many candies did Laura buy?

Laura's Candies = 5 + 3

Laura's Candies = 5 - 3

Here's a quick reminder of the steps you have learned:
Question | What's Known | Clue Words | Draw + Numbers | Equation

Write & Solve the Equation 1

Choose the correct equation. Use the blank space to work through the word problem steps.

Jim lined up four toy trucks and eight diggers. How many toys did he line up altogether?

> Total Toys = 4 + 8

> Total Toys = 8 - 4

Question | What's Known | Clue Words | Draw + Numbers | Equation

Write & Solve the Equation 1

Choose the correct equation. Use the blank space to work through the word problem steps.

A squirrel had twelve nuts in her nest. Her babies ate four of them. How many nuts are left?

Remaining Nuts = 12 + 4

Remaining Nuts = 12 - 4

Question | What's Known | Clue Words | Draw + Numbers | Equation

Write & Solve the Equation 1

Choose the correct equation. Use the blank space to work through the word problem steps.

Jan put eleven plates in the the dishwasher. She put five plates on the bottom shelf. How many plates did Jan put in the top shelf of the dishwasher?

Total Plates on Top Shelf = 11 + 5

Total Plates on Top Shelf = 11 - 5

Question | What's Known | Clue Words | Draw + Numbers | Equation

Write & Solve the Equation 2

Work through the steps to solve this equation. Write your answer at the bottom.

Simon planted 10 strawberry plants, but 4 died. How many strawberry plants does Simon have left?

Simon has _____ strawberry plants left.

Question | What's Known | Clue Words | Draw + Numbers | Equation

Write & Solve the Equation 2

Work through the steps to solve this equation. Write your answer at the bottom.

Sam washed five windows and Tina washed seven. How many windows did they wash in total?

Sam and Tina washed _____ windows.

Question | What's Known | Clue Words | Draw + Numbers | Equation

Write & Solve the Equation 2

Work through the steps to solve this equation. Write your answer at the bottom.

Trevor saved $9 then bought a book and now has $3 left. How much did the book cost?

The book cost _____.

Question | What's Known | Clue Words | Draw + Numbers | Equation

Write & Solve the Equation 2

Work through the steps to solve this equation. Write your answer at the bottom.

Tracey has 11 prizes and Timo has 9. How many more prizes does Timo need to match Tracey?

Question | What's Known | Clue Words | Draw + Numbers | Equation

Write & Solve the Equation 2

Work through the steps to solve this equation. Write your answer at the bottom.

The bookshelf has ten books. Rose took four books. How many books are left on the shelf?

Question | What's Known | Clue Words | Draw + Numbers | Equation

Part 2

Practice

Teacher Notes

Your student has now learned all the steps to solve a addition or subtraction word problem. In Part 2, your learner will practice these steps.

For the first four pages, the steps reminder will be included at the bottom of each page.

Word Problem Practice

Solve this word problem.

Gloria sang three sad songs and six happy songs. How many songs did she sing altogether?

Question | What's Known | Clue Words | Draw + Numbers | Equation

Word Problem Practice

Solve this word problem.

Teresa spent 6 minutes on the rowing machine and twelve minutes on the treadmill. How many minutes did she spend exercising?

Question | What's Known | Clue Words | Draw + Numbers | Equation

Word Problem Practice

Solve this word problem.

Victor mowed six lawns on Saturday and three lawns on Sunday. How many lawns did Victor mow overall?

Question | What's Known | Clue Words | Draw + Numbers | Equation

Word Problem Practice

Solve this word problem.

Vivian had ten dollars and then bought five dollars worth of fruit. How much money does Vivian have left?

Question | What's Known | Clue Words | Draw + Numbers | Equation

Word Problem Practice

Solve these word problems.

Kids at the beach built twelve sand castles, but then the tide washed away three of them. How many sand castles are left?

The teacher marked three exams, but she still has ten to go. How many exams does she have to mark in total?

Word Problem Practice

Solve these word problems.

Fido buried 7 bones in the back yard and 3 in the front yard. How many bones did he bury?

12 blocks fell out of the box onto the floor. Dora returned 7 of them to the box. How many blocks remain on the floor?

Word Problem Practice

Solve these word problems.

Sheila rolled two dice. One showed a 5 and the other was a 6. What do the dice add up to?

Dad washed three towels and four sheets. How many items did Dad wash?

Word Problem Practice

Solve these word problems.

A bee visited eight yellow flowers and twelve blue flowers. How many more blue flowers than yellow flowers did the bee visit?

This week, Ben needs to finish eleven lessons. He has already done five lessons. How many more lessons does he have to do?

Word Problem Practice

Solve these word problems.

Joanne has five crayons and Pippa has three more crayons than Joanne. How many crayons does Pippa have?

Bryan and James went for a drive. James drove 15 miles and James drove 12 miles. How many miles did they drive altogether?

Word Problem Practice

Solve these word problems.

Two nests contain twelve eggs in total. One nest contains 3 eggs. How many eggs are in the second nest?

It took 2 days for Peter to build a fence. On the first day he built 4 meters of the fence. On the second day he built another 4 meters of the fence. How long is the fence?

Word Problem Practice

Solve these word problems.

Kevin was 54 inches tall and then he grew another three inches. How tall is he now?

Jake folded nine items. Three were shirts and the rest were pants. How many pants did he fold?

Word Problem Practice

Solve these word problems.

Katy sent thirteen texts yesterday. She sent seven in the morning and the rest in the afternoon. How many did she send in the afternoon?

Shea watched three funny cat videos and four funny dog videos. How many videos did he watch altogether?

Word Problem Practice

Solve these word problems.

Clara counted the bottles of glue on the classroom bookshelf. There were 5 on the top shelf and three on the bottom shelf. How many bottles of glue were there altogether?

Shelly put eight books in a pile and then removed three of them. How many books are in the pile now?

Word Problem Practice

Solve these word problems.

Vivian caught nine insects and then let three go. How many does she have left?

The teacher's desk has two green pencils and three red pencils. How many pencils are on the teacher's desk?

Word Problem Practice

Solve these word problems.

Bert picked up two books off the floor and put them on the table. Three books remain on the floor. How many books were on the floor in the beginning?

Felip scored seven points and Rico scored nine points. How many more points does Felip need in order to tie with Rico?

Word Problem Practice

Solve these word problems.

Clara put three big plates and seven small plates on the table. How many plates did she put on the table in all?

Keith fed six pets. Three were dogs. How many pets did he feed that were not dogs?

Part 3

Extend

Teacher Notes

Congratulate your student on reaching so far in this workbook! They have done a great job.

In this section, your learner is given an answer to a word problem and their task is to write a math word problem that results in that answer.

This practice will really help your learner build critical thinking skills and cement their understanding of math word problems.

After some practice problems where there are no restrictions, your learner will then be challenged to write a word problem that specifically includes addition or subtraction.

Writing Word Problems

Write a word problem that results in this answer.

John has ten marbles.

Mary has seven flowers.

Writing Word Problems

Write a word problem that results in this answer.

There were ten fewer birds on the lake.

Fido planted three bones in the back yard.

Writing Word Problems

Write a word problem that results in this answer. Your word problem must involve addition.

There were seven chairs in the room.

John bought 15 candies altogether.

Writing Word Problems

Write a word problem that results in this answer. Your word problem must involve subtraction.

There were seven more red flowers than blue flowers.

Betty took three books.

Writing Word Problems

Write a word problem that results in this answer. Your word problem must involve addition.

Vicky bought five toys.

Jake ate seven slices of pizza.

Writing Word Problems

Write a word problem that results in this answer. Your word problem must involve subtraction.

Five of the cats were black.

Kyla mowed seven yards.

Congratulations on finishing the workbook!

You now know everything you need to know to complete many math word problems. Have fun being a word problem expert!

CERTIFICATE OF ACHIEVEMENT

THIS CERTIFICATE IS AWARDED TO

_____

IN RECOGNITION OF

_____

_____

DATE

_____

SIGNATURE

_____

TITLE

Printed in Great Britain
by Amazon